The Focus Booster

Booster

By Neil McNerney, MEd, LPC

The Focus Booster

The Focus Booster – Increase Your Focus In Five Easy Steps

ISBN 978-0-9839900-3-1

Published by:

Integrated Press
38878 Mt. Gilead Rd.
Leesburg, VA 20175
703-352-9002

Special Note:

Please remember that this book is not intended to give specific advice to your specific situation. Please consult a professional for specific advice. All names and stories in this book are composites and are not real people. Any similarities are purely coincidental.

DEDICATION

This book is dedicated to two of the most focused students I have ever met: Shannon McNerney and Max McNerney. I also dedicate this to my clients in my counseling practice. Your drive to improve your lives continues to be an inspiration.

Contents

Introduction

Why This Workbook?

The reason for this workbook is simple. No one has ever taught kids how to pay attention and stay focused. Grownups tell kids all the time: "Stay Focused, Pay Attention," but very few grownups have actually taught kids how to do it.

I have worked with students from kindergarten through college in the past 25 years and I have seen this same problem over and over: Kids don't know HOW to focus and pay attention.

Imagine that you are ten years-old and are going to swim for the very first time (I know, most ten year-old know how to swim, but work with me here). Your friend jumps in the deep end and starts swimming. He yells "Jump in" and you tell him you don't know how to swim. He says "Just start swimming!"

Do you see the ridiculousness of this? Telling someone how to swim by telling them to start swimming? It wouldn't work. In order to swim, you need a few lessons that begin with the basics.

Paying attention is the same way. Just telling you to pay attention is nowhere near enough information to get good at it.

In this workbook, I will share some tools about HOW to pay attention that you can use right away and for the rest of your life. You can even teach friends the tools, even your parents!

I Needed This When I Was A Kid

Confession time: When I was younger, I had a terrible time paying attention. I was pretty smart, so I did OK during elementary school. But by the time I hit middle school, I had lots of trouble paying attention. During a boring lecture, I would drift off almost immediately. I never fell asleep (thank goodness...I snore), but my mind would drift to a much more fun place.

Homework time was even harder for me, especially in high school. I could last about 5 or maybe 10 minutes before drifting off. I would get up, go see what's on TV, bug my sister (my older brother I never bugged...too big), and maybe go see what we were having for dinner. If I had the internet and facebook/twitter/ etc. back then, I would have been doomed.

I wish I could say that now, as an adult, I don't have trouble paying attention. But I still do. I am still easily distracted and can get off topic in a matter of minutes.

The difference now? I have learned some tools that help me stay focused and pay attention. Without these tools, I would be much more distracted.

Chapter 1
The Problem

- ✓ You are not lazy. Paying attention has nothing to do with laziness.
- ✓ Willpower is like a fuel tank, not like a muscle.

Just Try Harder!

You have probably heard it before: "Just try harder!" But the more you try, the harder it gets. Staying focused for a long time is <u>not</u> about trying harder. It's about finding a way to focus that doesn't completely tire you out.

You Aren't Lazy

Have you been called lazy recently? "Lazy" was a word I got used to when I was a student. "Neil? Well, he's smart, but he doesn't get his work done. He must be lazy." But I knew I wasn't lazy. A lazy person doesn't care. A lazy person just wants to lay around all day doing nothing. I was not lazy. But I couldn't pay attention to boring work for more than a few minutes before I started to drift off.

I don't care what other people say. You are not lazy. You just have trouble keeping focused on boring work.

Willpower is a Fuel Tank

This is a long story, but keep reading. It will explain why willpower is so hard to have sometimes. The story explains a huge part of this technique and shows why it works.

A group of researchers conducted an experiment on willpower, and the results were pretty surprising.

Imagine that you are a subject for a research study. You enter a small room with the researcher, and she asks you to have a seat in front of a table. She then sets two plates on the table. One plate has six or seven radishes. On the other plate are six or seven freshly baked chocolate chip cookies (emphasis on "freshly baked": they just came from the oven, still warm and smelling incredible!). Since you are a pretty smart person, you've already figured out that you will probably be randomly picked to eat either the radishes or the cookies. You are hoping for the cookies!

The experiment has already begun. You were right about being randomly picked, but you were unlucky. You were assigned the radishes. You are told to eat as many of the radishes as you would like, but to don't touch the cookies. The researcher then leaves the room, telling you she will be back in 10 minutes. Temptation now begins. Do I

eat the cookies? She told me to leave them alone. But they smell *so* good. But I want to be a good research subject. Back and forth your mind goes while you nibble on a bitter radish.

Ten minutes finally drags by and she escorts you to another room, where she asks you to attempt to solve a geometric puzzle, tracing a complicated shape without lifting your pencil or tracing again over a line. Unknown to you, this puzzle is designed to be impossible to solve. Eventually, in frustration, you give up, thinking that you have failed the experiment.

Willpower is like a fuel tank. When it's empty, there's nothing left.

While you were working on the puzzle, the researcher was timing how long it took you to give up. She added your time to the group of other radish eaters and compared the time with those participants who were told to eat cookies, as many as they wanted.

This last step, how long before a person gives up, is what was being measured. The cookie eaters try and try and try. On average, they take 19 minutes before giving up. The radish eaters? They last an average of 8 minutes! The radish eaters give up 11 minutes earlier than the cookie eaters! In the research field, that is a HUGE gap! Why?

The reason: The radish eaters ran out of willpower. They ran out of self-control. For 10 minutes in the first room, they had held back their impulses, keeping themselves from indulging in the cookies. So, by the time they got to the next room and were challenged again to control their impulse to give in (or give up), they gave up much quicker.

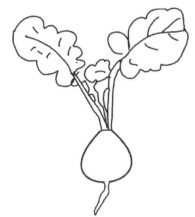

The radish eaters had depleted their ability to control themselves. What we now know about self-control is this: Self-Control is more like a fuel tank than a muscle. It can become depleted. And when it's depleted, it is very hard to have any willpower.

When you think about it, this makes a lot of sense. Think about when you have had a hard day and you come home to your family, how easy it is to snap at them. It's because we have tapped most our reserves of willpower during the day.

What does this mean for you? It means that for many, many of us, coming right home from school and getting our work out of the way will seem like an impossible task. It's because our willpower tank has been exhausted at school and we have nothing left when we get home.

Some students can take 20 or 30 minutes and are ready to go. If that's the case for you, fantastic. But many students, especially ones who might be struggling to get homework done, will probably need to take much longer, possibly up to an hour, before being ready to go at it again. Trying to get your homework done when your willpower tank is empty is very hard.

"I can't do it. My brain just feels like it's dead," is the statement of a student whose willpower tank is empty. What looks like laziness is often plain and simple exhaustion. Going to school, for many of us, is exhausting. What is exhausted? Our willpower.

So the idea to keep in mind is this: We need breaks, sometimes longer than we realize.

Remember:

✓ Self control is like a fuel tank. Don't let it hit empty.
✓ You can put fuel in your tank by doing relaxing and fun things.
✓ Small breaks can help increase your willpower.

Notes:

Chapter 2

The Timer

✓ What's so special about a timer?

✓ Where did this idea come from?

✓ How will this help keep my parents off my back?

What's So Special About a Timer?

Not much, actually. A timer is something that times things. But when used well, a timer can be a big deal. A timer, especially one of those old-school wind up kitchen timers, is a major piece of the puzzle to increase your focus. I'll tell you why the old-school timer works best in the next chapter.

Where Did This Idea Come From?

This idea came from a guy named Francesco Cirillo. He is guy in Italy who developed a program called The Pomodoro Technique. "Pomodoro" is Italian for "Tomato." Why a tomato? Well, the kitchen time he used was in the shape of a tomato, so he decided to name his technique "Pomodoro."

Although the Pomodoro Technique is good, I think it is much too complicated for most people, especially kids and teenagers (and many adults, including me).

How Will This Keep My Parents Off My Back?

It won't actually. But it will help. If your parents see that you are trying something new to improve your focus, they will love it. When they walk by your study area and see you with the Focus Chart and they hear the timer clicking, they will probably leave you alone. They will think something like, "Look at that! Evan's doing homework and using that new timer technique. That's great!" Hopefully they will keep walking and leave you alone!

Remember:

An old-school, windup kitchen timer is the one piece of equipment you will need for this workbook.

Notes:

Chapter 3

Forget about hours. Measure time in Boosters

✓ The "Booster" as a unit of time
✓ The Major Drift-Off
✓ The Timer

The Booster

The first step in using this technique is to begin the think about time in a different way. Instead of minutes or hours, we are going to develop a new unit of time: The Booster.

Minutes and hours are the same for everyone. We all have the same idea of how much time goes by in a minute, or in an hour. But a booster unit if time is different. It is a very personal unit of time:

One Booster is the amount of time you think you can stay focused on a boring project without getting really off task.

So you see, this amount of time will be different for different people. For example, your friend might be able to stay focused without distraction for 45 minutes, and for you it might be more like 10 minutes.

In fact, your own personal boosters might be different from day to day, hour to hour, or even from subject to subject. In the afternoon, you might be only able to stay focused for 10 minutes without drifting off, but in the morning you can stay focused for 20 minutes. You might also find that in certain subjects you can stay focused longer than others, so your booster time unit might be 15 minutes for math and 5 minutes for English.

Get it? It's a completely personal unit of time. The amount of time you think you can stay focused without a major drift-off.

What is a Major Drift Off?

When I say "Major Drift Off," I mean that you have gotten distracted and have completely stopped doing what you are supposed to be doing at that time. For example, as I was writing the last page, I have a few small drift off's. I looked at my Booster Timer a few times, said to myself "Man, I think the timer has stopped." But I kept writing. I was tempted to check facebook, but I didn't. I kept writing.

If I would have stopped writing and pulled up facebook, or checked my email, or got up to get a drink, then I would have had a Major Drift Off. So a Major drift off is when I stop what I am supposed to be doing and then find myself doing something unrelated to the task at hand.

We have minor drifts all the time, and we have fewer major drifts, but they happen. The goal of this technique is to reduce the major drifts.

The Timer

You will need a kitchen timer for this technique. Yes, the old-fashioned, turn the dial kind that you can get at just about any grocery store.

There is a reason for this. The old-fashioned timer makes a ticking sound as it counts down. This is an important part of why the technique works. As you do your homework, you will hear the ticking in the background. Believe it or not, that ticking sound will actually help you pay attention, for two reasons:

First, It's a bit distracting. A little bit of distraction are a good thing. Some recent research on study skills have shown that a small amount of distraction actually increases learning. Second, the tick, tick, tick is a reminder to keep focused. Every time your brain focuses on the ticking, you will remember to stay focused and not drift off, check the computer, etc.

So get yourself a timer, and make sure it's the old-fashioned kind.

Remember:

Hours and minutes are for your parents. Measure time in boosters.

Notes:

Chapter 4

The Quick and Dirty Method

Start Studying and Track Distractions

Although the complete method is very powerful, it's a bit complicated. I would suggest you try the Quick and Dirty Method first to see how you like it. The Q&D method only focuses on short periods of intense focus, followed by short breaks.

You will need page 2 of the Study Sheet (p. 42). Here is what the first row looks like:

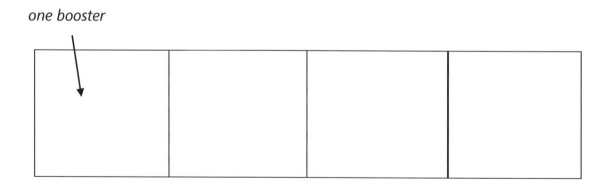

one booster

Each of those squares equals one booster. A booster is a short period of time where you will try your hardest to stay focused. I would suggest, at the beginning, that you use 10 minutes as the amount of time you will use for each booster.

Set the timer to your booster unit (for our example, 10 minutes) and begin your work. Go about it just like you usually would, but try not to give in to any distractions.

Every time you notice that you have drifted off, put a mark in the box. For example: You are working on your math problems and it's going well, but you see your drinking out of his bowl and you think "I'm thirsty too. I wonder if I can sneak in the kitchen and grab a soda."

Once you notice you are not focusing, put a mark in square and get back to work! You will be able to sneak a soda when the timer rings.

When the timer rings, take a five minute break. Set the timer for five minutes and relax.

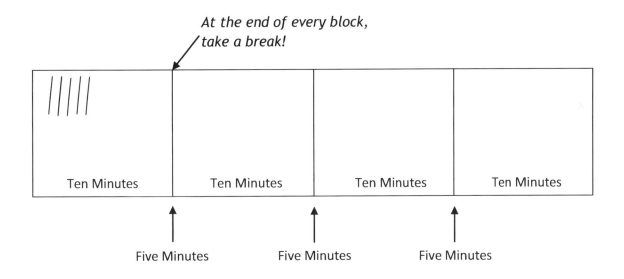

Take The Breaks!

Take a break even if you feel like one yet. If you wait until you feel like you need a break, it's too late. You have emptied your willpower fuel tank (see Chapter 6 – The Fuel Tank). When you empty your willpower fuel tank, it becomes harder and harder to get work done and stay focused.

What should you do during a break?

- ✓ Get a snack.
- ✓ Sneak a soda.
- ✓ Go bug your sister.
- ✓ Ask dad what's for dinner.
- ✓ Ask mom if you can go over your friend's house later.
- ✓ Text your friends.
- ✓ Do some pushups.
- ✓ Run around the yard.
- ✓ Play with your dog.
- ✓ Read your favorite book.

You get the idea. The break should be something that you can start and stop within five minutes.

What should you <u>not</u> do during the break?

- χ Turn on the TV.
- χ Play a video game.
- χ Go outside and play with friends.
- χ Take a bath.
- χ Cut the grass.

All of these things will either last more than five minutes, or they will be very hard to stop after five minutes (except maybe cutting the grass). Good luck just playing a video game for five minutes and being able to stop when the timer dings!

After the five minute break, set the timer for ten minutes and start working again, putting marks into the next box on the sheet of paper.

Yes, I know what you are thinking. If you take a five minute break after every ten minutes, it might take you forever to get your work done. But that won't be the case. In fact, it will probably take less time since you are working at a much more intense level. If ten minutes seems very easy for you, then increase it to fifteen minutes and see how that works.

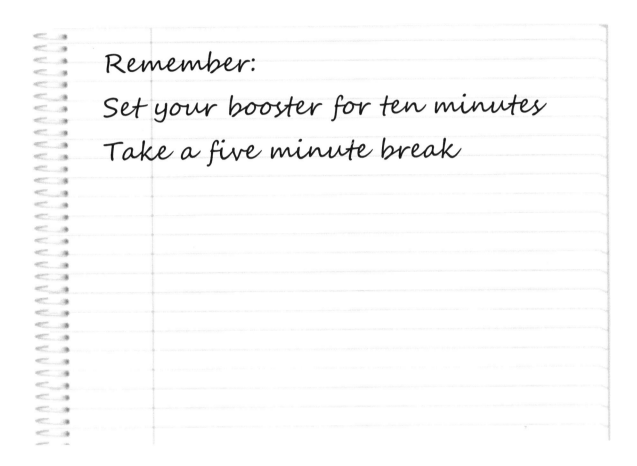

Remember:

Set your booster for ten minutes

Take a five minute break

Chapter 5

How to do it – The Full Process

✓ The Five Step Plan

Now that you understand the plan, let's see how it works in real life. I will take a standard homework night and work through all of the steps, one by one.

I will be easier to follow along by tearing out Worksheet #1, which we will be using for this example. Don't worry: there are many more spare worksheets in the back of this workbook. If you would rather not tear it out, go to thefocusbooster.com/handouts for more worksheets you can print.

Step 1 – List all the Tasks

The first step in using Boosters is listing all of the work you have to get done during the study period. I will make up a situation and write down the information.

After each example, there is a place for you to write your own information. Go ahead and write it in the book. It's a workbook, for Pete's sake.

For instance, let's say it's Tuesday night and you have the following work to do:

English: *Read 20 pages, finish first draft of opinion paper*

Math: *p. 324, even problems 2-8, study for chapter 13 quiz*

Band: *Practice 20 minutes*

Science: *Finish 'elements worksheet'*

Write your homework here:

Subject 1

_____

Subject 2

_____

Subject 3

_____

Subject 4

_____

Now, separate the homework by tasks, not by subjects. In the list above, there are four subjects, but how many tasks? Let's circle each task:

English: (Read 20 pages) (finish first draft of opinion paper)

Math: (p. 324, even problems 2-8) (study for chapter 13 quiz)

Band: (Practice 20 minutes)

Science: (Finish 'elements worksheet')

Count the circles: _6_ . So there are 6 tasks for tonight's homework.

You will then write them down in the Booster Sheet (more about that later) with one task per line:

#	Task	Boosters
	English - read 20 pages	
	English - finish first draft of opinion paper	
	Math – p. 324, even problems 2-28	
	Math - study for chapter 13 quiz for ten minutes	
	Band - Practice 20 minutes	
	Science – Finish 'elements worksheet'	

Now, go back to your subjects that you wrote above and circle the number of tasks you have to do tonight. Remember: one class might have more than one task.

Put *your* tasks in the worksheet below:

#	Task	Boosters

Did you notice that I only added the tasks? I didn't put a number in the left hand column, and I didn't put anything in the 'booster' column. There is a reason for that. It's something we will add in a minute.

Step 2 – Estimate Your Attention Span

In this step, you will estimate your attention span. By "attention span," I mean the amount of time you think you can stay focused without a major drift-off.

For instance:

- If you are pretty well rested, you might think you could go for 15 minutes without of major drift off.
- If you know this is going to be a tough evening to stay focused, you might estimate 10 minutes.

- If you have an amazing level of attention, you might use 20 minutes. But if you have an amazing level of attention span, why are you reading this book anyway?

Here is a good estimate based on age and how distractible you might be. This is just an estimate. Your mileage may vary.

Age	Minutes Well Focused	Minutes Easily Distracted
8-10	10	8
11-13	12	10
14-15	15	10
16-adult	18	10

I am an easily distracted person, and when I am feeling well-focused, the best I can do is 18 minutes. I usually set my boosters for 15 minutes. Sometimes I have to set them for 10 minutes when I am tired and easily distracted.

You will quickly figure out your upper and lower numbers after you have used the technique for a while.

Your Booster Unit

Write down how many minutes you will be using per booster for this homework session and write it down at the top of the worksheet. For example, let's say you think you could go 10 minutes without a major drift off:

Booster Unit: **10 minutes**

#	Task	Minutes	Boosters
	English - read 20 pages		

Write Your Booster Unit Here: Booster Unit: _____minutes

Step 3 – Estimate Booster Units

Now comes the estimating part. An estimate is your best guess on how long each task will take. Since we are using 10 minutes as the booster unit, let's keep our estimates at ten minute blocks.

Let's say that reading 20 pages might take you 30 minutes. If your booster unit is ten minutes long, then the reading assignment will take 3 booster units.

So we just need to do the math: 30 minutes divided by 10 booster minutes = 3 boosters

Write the number of minutes per task here

#	Task	Minutes	Boosters
	English - read 20 pages	30	3
	English - finish first draft of opinion paper	10	1
	Math – p. 324, even problems 2-8	10	1
	Math - , study for chapter 13 quiz	10	1
	Band - Practice 20 minutes	20	2
	Science – Finish 'elements worksheet'	20	2

Write the number of boosters for each task here

Go back to the top of page 14 and write the estimated time for each task and then convert them into booster units. Go ahead and do it now. I'll wait right here.

Do this for each task. For example, the opinion paper might take ten minutes. Same with the math and studying for the math quiz. So these three tasks each will take one booster. Band practice for twenty minutes equals two boosters, and science will take twenty minutes, which equals two boosters.

Step 4 – Rank the Homework

This next piece of advice might sound different than you are used to: Start your homework with the **easiest** task, then the hardest task, then the rest in any order you like.

There is a very important, scientific reason for this. When we begin a boring set of tasks by doing the easiest (or most enjoyable) first, it gets us started and increases our motivation to get the rest done.

A lot of times, when it comes to homework, the hardest part is getting started. If that's the case, why not make it easy to get started by doing the easy stuff first?

There has been a ton of research on this concept. Start with the easy stuff first to get yourself motivated. But when, then, do I suggest you do the hardest one second instead of last? I think you know the reason: If you save it for the last, you might not get to it. Your willpower might have completely faded by that point.

So look over the list and rank them, but start with the easiest. Let's assume you are fantastic a math, the science worksheet is almost complete, and band practice is easy. But you hate English, especially writing papers.

This is how your ranking might look:

Math is the easiest, so do it first!
English is the hardest, so do it second!

#	Task	Minutes	Boosters
5	*English - read 20 pages*	30	3
2	*English - finish first draft of opinion paper*	10	1
1	*Math – p. 324, even problems 2-28*	10	1
6	*Math - , study for chapter 13 quiz*	10	1
3	*Band - Practice 20 minutes*	20	2
4	*Science – Finish 'elements worksheet'*	20	2

Do the same for your own chart on page 14. Rank by difficulty starting with the easiest, then the hardest, then the rest.

Step 4 – Start Studying and Track Distractions

Now is the time to start the studying, finally! I know; it seems like we spent a lot of time planning, but trust me, it will help a lot and it will go quicker once you get used to the plan.

Do you see all of the squares at the bottom of the page? Good. Each of those squares equals one booster.

one booster

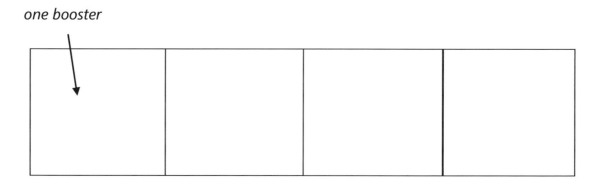

Set the timer to your booster unit (for our example, 10 minutes) and begin your work. Go about it just like you usually would, but try not to give in to any distractions.

Every time you notice that you have drifted off, put a mark in the box. For example: You are working on your math problems and it's going well, but you see your sister go get a snack and you think "I'd like a snack. I wonder what she got? I'm going to get something too."

Once you notice you are not focusing, put the mark in square and get back to work! You will be able to get up for a snack when the timer rings.

When the timer rings, take a four or five minute break. Set the timer for five minutes and relax.

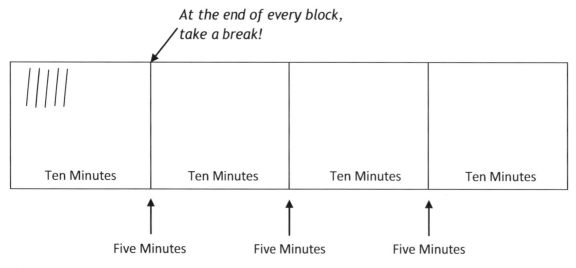

Step 5 – Take The Breaks!

This is a very important part of the plan. Take a break even if you feel like one yet. If you wait until you feel like you need a break, it's too late. You have emptied your willpower fuel tank (see Chapter 6 – The Fuel Tank).

When you empty your willpower fuel tank, it becomes harder and harder to get work done and stay focused.

What should you do during a break?

- ✓ Get that snack.
- ✓ Go bug your sister.
- ✓ Ask dad what's for dinner.
- ✓ Ask mom if you can go over your friend's house later.
- ✓ Text your friends.
- ✓ Do some pushups.
- ✓ Run around the yard.
- ✓ Play with your dog.
- ✓ Read your favorite book.

You get the idea. The break should be something that you can start and stop within five minutes.

What should you not do during the break?

Turn on the TV. Play a video game. Go outside and play with friends. Take a bath. Cut the grass.

All of these things will either last more than five minutes, or they will be very hard to stop after five minutes (except maybe cutting the grass). Good luck just playing a video game for five minutes and being able to stop when the timer dings!

Notes:

Chapter 6
Paying Attention in School During Boring Lectures

You know the feeling. It's after lunch and you had three slices of pizza. You have a history lecture, and your teacher is beyond dull. You forgot the tape to keep your eyelids open. You might die of boredom. What do you do? The Focus Booster idea can easily be adjusted to use during boring times at school. Try using these steps:

Prepare for the boring class

Drink – Water preferably. A big gulp of water can increase your alertness. Try to drink 8 ounces. At a water fountain, each swallow is about an ounce. Try drinking 8 swallows of water. Anything else but water will cause you more problems very quickly. Soda, even juice, has a lot of sugar in it, which will produce a quick bolt of energy followed quickly by a drop in concentration. Caffeine does the same thing. It will boost your concentration for a little while, then your concentration will drop.

Get Cold – Take off your sweatshirt or coat, even splash some water on your face. If your skin temperature is high, you will be more sleepy and less focused.

Get Uncomfortable – It's hard to drift off when you are uncomfortable. The easiest way to do this is this: don't use the back of your chair. Instead of leaning, or slouching, on the back of your chair, try sitting as if it's a bench. Have you ever seen someone fall asleep while sitting on a bleacher? I haven't. It's impossible.

Go to the Head of the Class – If you are having trouble staying focused, move to the front. Yes, the front. Right next to the teacher. It will be much harder to drift off with the teacher right next to you.

Make a Quick Booster Chart

First figure out how much time you have left in the period. For this example, let's say that there is 40 minutes left.

Second divide the time left (40 minutes) by 10. 40/10=4

Third make a quick booster chart with 4 squares. Then take a look at the clock and enter the time in each square, adding ten minutes for each square:

1:15 |||	1:25	1:35	1:45

Then start tracking your drift offs.

Every time you drift off, make a mark in the box. After the first ten minutes, start using the next box, and so on.

No, you won't be able to take the five minute breaks between each ten minute block. Your teacher might not approve if you got up and ran around the room for five minutes. But I promise you that this tool will make it much easier to stay focused and will also make the time go quicker.

Chapter 7
Just the FAQ's

✓ Frequently Asked Questions

I don't have a kitchen timer. Can I use another type of timer?

Sure. But if you have a kitchen timer, it tends to work best. There is something about the tick tick tick of the wind up timer that helps to remind you to stay focused.

My brother (dog, pet iguana) interrupts me. Is that a drift off?

Yes, it is. See what you can do to have your parents help you keep everyone away from you. If you are trying something new to help you stay focused, they will probably help keep the annoying family members away.

I ran out of sheets, now what?

Go to: thefocusbooster.com/worksheets - You will find copies that you can print.

My parents keep checking in on me, which makes me drift, what should I do?

Write this on a piece of paper and give it to them:

> *Mom and Dad,*
> *I am trying to use this new focus booster idea, but every time you come in to check on me, I drift off and have to put a mark in the box. Could you please not come in so much? Thanks.*

When should I increase my booster time?

When you are seeing that you only have one or two marks in each box, it's probably time to increase the booster time. But don't increase it more than 5 minutes at a time. Also, don't be surprised if you never increase it. I can only do about fifteen minutes maximum.

I've used this tool for a while, but I'm getting bored with it. Now what?

I can relate. Whenever I try a new technique, it works for a few weeks, and then I begin to get bored. I then use it less and less until I completely forget about it.

When you begin to be bored with this, stop using it immediately for a few days, but give yourself a reminder to go back to it after 4 or 5 days. I know, strange advice, but I find that stopping for a few days works much better than trying to push through the boredom.

You will see that if you return to the technique after a few days, you won't be as bored with it and you might be able to use it for even longer without becoming bored.

Notes:

Chapter 8
New Research On Attention

- ✓ Some distractibility can be a good thing
- ✓ Doing homework the same time every day might work
- ✓ Don't worry so much about what type of learner you are

There has been a ton of new research on study skills and paying attention. The trouble is that very few teachers and parents know about it. In this section, I hope to make you an expert on attention so that you will be able to tell your parents exactly how you can best study.

But go easy on them. Your parents mean well. They want exactly the same thing you do. They want you to be successful in school. Although their definition of success might be different than your definition (straight A's?), you and your parents have the same goal.

Some of the material in this chapter might seem unusual, and might be completely different than other advice you have been given. But you also might have an "I knew it!" moment as well. When I researched this information, I kept thinking to myself "This makes complete sense. No wonder the typical techniques didn't work for me." So keep you mind open as you read this. I'll list them as myths.

Myth #1: Study in a Quiet Place

We have all heard this one a million times. Find a quiet place to study, free from distractions—that way, you can focus on your work. This piece of advice works for many people...except the people it doesn't work for.

This piece of advice is repeated over and over by those people who like having a quiet place to study (Their reasoning might sound something like "Since it works for me, it should work for everyone").

In fact, many of us do much better when there is some type of sound going on. For some of us, the idea of studying in a quiet place will drive us nuts! It's quiet, too quiet. Some distractions can be helpful, such as:

✓ someone in the kitchen
✓ music
✓ traffic in the background
✓ even a 'sound machine' is helpful

Some of us would rather do their schoolwork in the kitchen, or the dining room near "the action." More and more research is showing that this is the case. A few words of caution, though:

Don't have the music too loud, for two reasons: One – it needs to be the secondary focus of your attention, not the primary focus. Two – even if you convince your parents that it's OK to listen, they will still yell at you to turn down that racket if it's too loud.

TV still tends to be the deal breaker. Although not yet certain, it's pretty clear that television provides too much of a distraction and doesn't enhance learning. But music, background conversation, or similar white noise might be just the ticket for certain learners.

Myth #3 – Study in the Same Place at the Same Time

Create a study spot, have all of the necessary materials at the same place, and have a routine that allows you to do homework at the same time every day.

In my opinion, this can be a recipe for failure, for more than one reason.

First, most research about learning is telling us that students learn better when they learn and study the material in many locations. We have actually known this for 30 years!

In one experiment, college students who studied a list of 40 vocabulary words in different rooms—one windowless and cluttered, the other modern, did much better on a test than students who studied the words in the same room. By the way, the initial study was done in 1978!

This is an example of how certain ideas are hard to break, even if there is little evidence to back them up. Possibly one of the reasons it has remained so popular is that doing things in the same place/same time is very convenient for the parents!

My suggestion: Add variety to the places where you are studying. If you can read in the car without getting carsick, great. Students spend much more time in the car these days than in years past. It's a great place to study vocabulary, spelling, do math homework, etc. Are your parent's cooking dinner? Have them quiz you on your flashcards while you help fix the meal, or set the table. Watching TV? Use the commercial breaks to memorize biology terms.

The second part of the myth, studying at the same time every day, has no evidence that it does any good. I am pretty convinced that most of the articles suggesting this are written by authors who are naturally very organized and think their routines will work for everyone.

My experience with so many struggling students tells me that we are setting them up for failure by trying to get them to study in a way that is strongly against their nature. I have rarely seen a child who doesn't naturally gravitate toward a schedule and then adopt it wholeheartedly.

This advice is additionally hard because, if you live in a typical modern family, no two days of the week are the same. Telling students to have the same routine each day of the week is a double failure. One: It doesn't work because our lives are too different from day to day, and two: It's something that we will feel bad about when we can't make it happen.

Suggestion: Study when you have the time. Many middle and high schools have resource time. Use it. It's a bit distracting, with your friends nearby, but a bit of distraction is a good thing, right? Boring bus ride home? Do your required reading.

Myth #4: I Need to Learn Based on My Learning Style

I recently had the pleasure of visiting a local elementary classroom where the kids were having a great time with a spelling project. They had gone outside and collected twigs and were now in the process of gluing the twigs to construction paper in the shapes of letters to make their spelling list. It was a fun, messy project, and I wished I'd had a teacher like that when I was a kid. When I asked her about the activity, she told me it was to help the kids learn by using their kinesthetic sense of learning. By touching the letter shapes, it will help them learn their spelling words.

"Plus, it's a lot of fun! We have been cooped up in this room too long with bad weather. We needed to get outside for a while."

I could tell that it certainly was fun. But I was very skeptical that the kids were actually learning anything about their spelling words by touching the twigs.

For the past 20+ years, a certain theory of learning has become so widespread that most people accept it as fact: Students have specific learning styles. Most of the time, we talk about three major styles: Auditory (hearing the information), Visual (seeing the information), and Kinesthetic (touching, moving, etc.). The theory then states that each student has a major strength in one of the areas, and that it is the job of the parents and teachers to help students learn based on their area of strength.

There is a bit of truth to this myth. Just like in any comparison to others, we all will fall on a bell curve based on where our strengths lie. But most of us will fall pretty close to the center line.

So, if the theory is wrong, why is it that everyone thinks it's right? One reason is that almost everyone believes it, not just educators. Up to 90 percent of college students know about this theory and accept it as fact (Willingham, 2009). However, there is some truth to the theory. Some of us have a specific method for learning that is better than others. But most of us still fall within a pretty narrow range of average.

In Dr. Willingham's words (Willingham, 2005):

> "What cognitive science has taught us is that children do differ in their abilities with different modalities, but **teaching the** child in his best modality doesn't affect his educational achievement. What does matter is whether the child is taught in the content's best modality."

What this means is that the method of teaching should be predicated on the subject matter, instead of trying to customize the teaching to the student who is being taught. For instance, spelling is taught best through the visual channel: seeing the words on the paper.

When spelling is taught via the auditory channel (hearing the words), learning declines. What is remembered is the tone of voice, not the actual words. Try teaching a child the shape of his home state by describing it verbally! It's very hard. Even if you give a child a piece of wood shaped like the state, he will still be remembering it via his "mind's eye." He will be making a picture of it in his head.

What does this mean to us? Mainly, relax about trying to figure out your learning style. It won't make much of a difference when it comes to actual learning. Also, don't try to structure your study routine based on learning style. It tends to be not as helpful as you might think and saps your-already depleted amount of willpower.

So when it comes to the things we know about studying, give yourself some room to think outside the box. Just because a certain study style worked for your parents doesn't mean it will work for you.

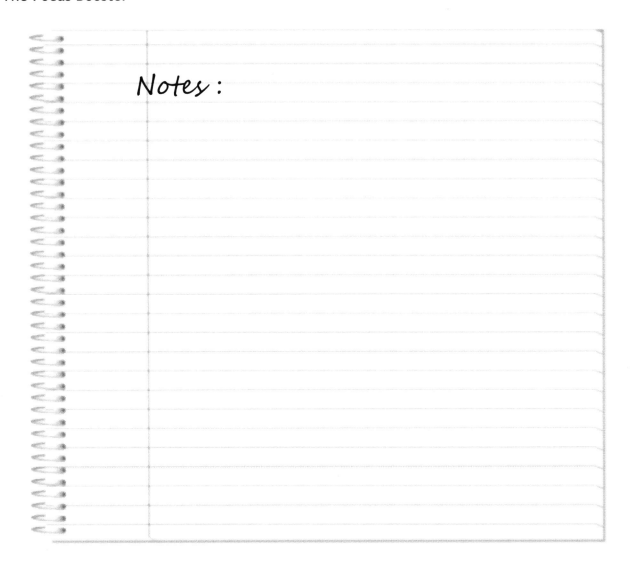

Notes :

Chapter 9
Sample Worksheets

The Focus Booster
Daily Homework Sheet

Page 1

Date: _____   Booster Unit: _____mins.

Order	Task	Minutes	Boosters

The Focus Booster

Daily Homework Sheet

Page 2

Time for each Booster _____   Time for each break _____

The Focus Booster
Daily Homework Sheet

Page 1

Date: _____   Booster Unit: _____mins.

Order	Task	Minutes	Boosters

The Focus Booster

Daily Homework Sheet

Page 2

Time for each Booster _____   Time for each break _____

The Focus Booster
Daily Homework Sheet

Page 1

Date: _____   Booster Unit: _____mins.

Order	Task	Minutes	Boosters

The Focus Booster

Daily Homework Sheet

Page 2

Time for each Booster _____   Time for each break _____

The Focus Booster
Daily Homework Sheet

Page 1

Date: _____   Booster Unit: _____mins.

Order	Task	Minutes	Boosters

The Focus Booster

Daily Homework Sheet

Page 2

Time for each Booster _____   Time for each break _____

The Focus Booster
Daily Homework Sheet

Page 1

Date: _____   Booster Unit: _____mins.

Order	Task	Minutes	Boosters

The Focus Booster

Daily Homework Sheet

Page 2

Time for each Booster _____   Time for each break _____

Chapter 10
A Note to Parents

How to Get Buy-In from Your Kids

I would guess that it was you who probably bought this book for your kids, but how can you actually get them to read it? Here are some ideas:

Leave it lying around.

I know, not a very subtle technique, but it works pretty well. If you leave it lying around the house, they might actually pick it up. When they ask about it, don't be too excited. "It's something I picked up. Take a look and let me know what you think."

Don't make them read it.

Don't start with a requirement that they read it. If you do, they might read it, but they won't be interested in implementing the techniques. Giving them a choice will increase the chances that they will actually use it.

Read it yourself and try some of the techniques.

By telling them that you have tried some of the ideas and it has really helped, it gives your stamp of approval and it also tells them that you have trouble staying focused from time to time.

Be tentative when talking about it.

Try saying things like:

"I don't know if this would help you or not."
"You might have already tried something like this, but..."
"This seems like a really good idea. I'd love to know what you think."

Show them the videos

Kids are much more likely to consider something by watching a YouTube clip first. Send them the YouTube links as a way to get their interest: thefocusbooster.com/youtube

Resources

Timers and Sound Machines

I put together an Amazon store where you can find my recommended timers, sound machines and books. You can find it here: thefocusbooster.com/timers

Videos

Go to my YouTube page to see some videos explaining the Focus Booster Method:
thefocusbooster.com/youtube

Questions?

Don't hesitate to email me: neil@neilmcnerney.com

Acknowledgments

I would like to give special thanks to all the students who have helped me practice this technique. I have learned quite a bit on what works and what doesn't when it comes to focusing. Most of that was due to the hard work of students who want to become better focused.

Thanks to my family, Colleen, Shannon, and Max, for their patience as I have worked on this workbook. I have spent too many days, nights and weekends holed up trying to put these ideas in print.

Thanks to those who have supported my writing projects, especially my mother Dorothy McNerney.

Thanks to my colleagues who have been great supporters of both my clinical work and my writing, including John Milliken, Kathleen Marshall, Pam Brott, Peg Dale, Emily Goodman Scott, Angela Gwyn Atwater, Susan McCormick, Sue Simpson, and Tammy Davis.

Thanks to my administrators, Tiffany Jenkins and Lauren Kruck, who have helped keep me sane by doing all of the detail work of my life.

Made in the USA
Lexington, KY
19 November 2014